VICTORIA HUTCHINSON

HEART CALL

POETIC CONVERSATIONS WITH GOD

innovo
PUBLISHING
innovopublishing.com

Published by Innovo Publishing, LLC
www.innovopublishing.com
1-888-546-2111

innovo
PUBLISHING
innovopublishing.com

Publishing Books, eBooks, Audiobooks, Music, Screenplays, & Courses for the
Christian & wholesome markets since 2008.

HEART CALL
Poetic Conversations with God

Library of Congress Control Number: 2023923926
ISBN: 978-1-61314-981-2

Cover Design & Interior Layout: Innovo Publishing, LLC

Printed in the United States of America
U.S. Printing History
First Edition: 2024

Has God called you to create a Christ-centered or wholesome book, eBook,
audiobook, music album, screenplay, or online course? Visit Innovo's educational
center (cpportal.com) to learn how to accomplish your calling with excellence.

INTRODUCTION

As time passes, I'm starting to understand what it means to be alive. And, as much as I would like to say it's just inhaling and exhaling, it's not. It's not working to make the means to survive here on this earth. It's not making a lifetime of plans by which you may or may not accomplish, and it's not accumulating awards that are only marveled for a moment. I have learned that all those things just help us survive. It helps bring meaning to our own individual lives.

But, over the last decade of my life, I have spent time getting to know the Author of this life. I have spent hours in God's love which, in turn, became my lifeline. I have spent years trying to understand this great mercy to see all the beauty His hands have created. And I haven't felt so alive until the day He took hold of my heart. Where grace didn't just change the course of my thoughts and the decisions I would make but ultimately the path I would take.

So when I said I'm starting to understand what it means to be alive, it's because this heart could receive signals, signs, and supplements from any place—but I received a call from the Father who not only knows me but created me. When He called, He gave me some words that I thought were just to encourage myself. But these words were given to inspire, encourage, and provide an opportunity for us all to answer God's call. A call to live. A call directly from God.

LIFE AFTER DEATH

◆

The sound,
The very sight.
It was the one thought that turned my life around,
The one color that I see shine bright.
This image brought me to tears;
It stops my heartbeat.
The very sight is so vague and clear
That my heart turns as black as the street.
You said you wanted to see me break,
Wanted to see my whole body shake.
Then let me begin to create
This very memory that isn't hard to make.
I was dead,
Not in a deep trance,
And my thoughts were easily read,
And my skin was about to prance.
The floor was lava,
My body began to burn.
I began to scream, "Mama."
I felt my whole body turn.
The flames attacked my body;
My skin began to peel.
No longer did I feel like a little miss hottie.
I just wanted my body to heal.
One by one my flesh began to fall
And no longer could I stand tall.
My bones were so bare,
And I lost all my hair.
This was torture.
I knew where I was—in hell.
How could I go away from my culture?
All I could do was yell.

Slowly my body began to disintegrate.
My body was just bones; all my skin was dripping like blood.
I was in eternal suffering,
And all I could hear was others moan.
I laid there feeling the fire devour me
Until I felt my bones and skin mend.
I stood in a gorgeous room made of gold, and before me stood *her*
In the most outstanding gown
And the fullest wings.
Her eyes no longer weary
But full of joy.
I stood there with my eyes teary.
All I could say was, "Oh."
It was my grandma.
I haven't seen her in years,
Probably because she was dead,
And she never dropped tears.
I reached out to try to touch her
When a gate just appeared.
All I could think was, "Why?"
Heaven was in my reach.
Who wants to see me broken?
I knew it was over,
And heaven was my last token.
I lived my life and lost it while I was undercover,
But I didn't want my grandma to see what I've become—a criminal,
Lost in all my thoughts that were idiotic and subliminal.

I couldn't do this again.
I dropped to my knees.
I screamed, "God, I learned my lesson, please."
Tears rolled down my cheeks.
Inside my soul was so meek.
Living in a world where I can't determine whether I'm coming or going,
In hell or heaven,
Living in a castle or cavern,
Breathing or slowly dying,
Smiling or just crying.
Trying or giving up,
Standing or just falling apart,
Seeing in light or dark,
Fearless or fearful.
Figuring out whether I could live with or without,
Believing that I'll learn to dance.
But unfortunately, I lost my last chance
To give,
Not to just live.
Where will you go?
And it's sad if you don't know.

———✦———

LIFE AFTER DEATH: SIGNS OF GOD'S COMING

I've shared a previous experience on death,
And if I may express another which has taken place?
I heard it clear as day:
The ringing of bells,
The loud car crashes,
Wailing of mothers as their children vanished.
The loss of aerodynamics as a phone plummeted towards a
destination
Unmarked.
The birds of the air screeched in a uniform clan,
And at that moment the earth began to creak,
The houses began to crumble on a rhythmic streak.
The earth opened its mouth and belched immense fire.
I stood motionless
As I watched the hour of the Rapture occur.
I was snapped out of my trance by a group of freed dogs which
Attacked and ripped the flesh of a woman carrying her wounded baby.
The blood dripped from their mouths aimlessly,
And as their eyes turned to me,
I took this as a perfect invitation to flee.
I ran with all
Might and purpose
To get to a secure destination
Before I was to meet a tragic assassination.
Coming to a house with no indents,
I entered in,
Heart pounding,
Eyes racing to recognize any traps
Lying around to terrorize and thwart my exterior.
I sat down to gather my mind,

But all I could think was what caused me to be left here
To suffer around in this eerie chaotic soundless world.
Surely my life was in God's will.
Surely my name would be etched in the Book of Life—
With no darken lines but with a clear permanent seal.
Surely God has made a mistake,
Or maybe this was truly to be my fate.
"Surely God didn't leave me," I cried.
"Surely I was just a little late."
"Surely I was meant to go."
Then, at that moment, it dawned on me: the Lord had come
And gone.
I was to fend for myself.
I knew not where I was,
For all around me loud boisterous voices could be heard.
Before I knew it,
The door flung open.
Men with strange armor marched in,
Snatched my living body, then threw me into a truck.
Inside the truck were many teenagers like myself,
Each one more terrified than the next.
I began to pray,
"God, I know You hear all.
Please, God, answer my deepest pleading call."
Tears rolled down my cheeks;
I felt my insides groan.
Then all at once my blood and soul calmed.
I opened my eyes and the others looked in shock.
I responded to their astonishment,
"God will save us."

One boy stood up and spoke:
"Who are you to tell us who will rescue us
When I watched my mother and sister vanish?
Once there, then nothing, not even a shadow.
And now I'm here, going to a place that's 'safe.'
So please tell me how this 'God' can do anything."

In simultaneous glares, all the teens looked back at me.
I had no words to give them hope,
And the few I tried to voice were silenced
By rapid gun shots.
Then the truck jerked to a stop.
"Get out," a loud voice boomed.
Each child fumbled, one after the other.
I slowly stepped out into the blazing light.
All around me were burning crosses and Bibles.
The more we walked, blood stains deepened with each plight.
Then a small crowd began to assemble,
Each person who wore a facade more fervently reprimanding than the
last.
We all were forced onto a stage
To face the endless crowd we assumed had passed.
When I climbed the steps, the crowd seemed to expel their rage.
Tears rolled down my face, for I knew not what I did.
All I wanted was to go home.
Groups of men came up,
And each asked us, "Do you believe in God?"
One by one each teen seemed to renounce their original answer.
Coming to me now, the soldier demanded my plea.
I responded,
"Yes, I do."
The crowd's voice became a monotonous, eerie sea.
The teens by my side took the mark,
Then fleeted as if escaping gave them moral meaning.
The soldiers aimed their guns at me
And one by one relinquished rounds of ammo into my body.
One pierced my thigh; I screamed in agony.
Another was from afar, attacking my shoulder.
One from close up sliced through my abdomen, as another
Hugged my spinal cord.
I hit the floor, unable to feel the blood expelling

From my body or the few breaths inside.
The soldier which stood in front of my paralyzed body
Laughed methodically, then signaled for the other soldiers to
Cease fire.

"Do you still believe in this God,
An alleged God who let you lay in a pool of your
Own blood?
A God who will watch us murder numerous more,
Then throw away as useless sod?
What kind of God is that?
If He shall not save you, then who and when?
Your God exists not, and neither will you."

He aimed his gun at my heart.
As he fired the final blow, I recoiled my final words:
"I do!"
The bullet plummeted through my ribcage
And stabbed into my heart.
As I felt my heartbeats cease slowly,
My eyes dropped their final ounce of life.
I died.

There's not much that needs to be said,
So, I'll leave you with a thought
Instead.
If you see the signs,
Get right with God
Because He is coming.
I'm pretty sure you would rather
Be taken than left behind—
And dead.

GIVE ME YOU

If all I see is in front of me,
Take away these eyes
So I can see with my heart,
Not with wondering sight.
If all I have can only be held
In these hands of mine,
Open the creases and folds
That limit the things I control.
And Lord, recreate an abundant flood
If these ears hear words of doubt.
Silence the canal that leads to my thoughts
And resurrect the very meaning of my life.
To praise and shout
If this heart beats without Your command
Or shields hurt that You could heal
By just the utterance of Your voice.
Destroy every hurt like quicksand,
And recreate a fresh love from above.
If my plans seem
To be bounded by greed
And selfish ambition
Like a guilty convict,
Fill my body with conviction,
Where every being in me would
Search for redirection.
If this body of mine

Grows weak along the journey,
Let the bright rays of Your love
Brighten and uplift me every morning.
God, place an unction in me
That begs for oxygen like a red blood cell.
Plant vital elements of Your Word
So through time all can tell.
Place in me a pledge of allegiance
To a King who is You,
That through perils and plight
I know Your love for me would withstand
Vengeance.
God, like Solomon,
I ask for the ways of You.
I ask for the heart of You
To be able to love as You do,
Knowing when it's better to walk as one or two.
To reach hearts that feel as if You
Left falling apart.
God, like the clouds in the sky,
Fill me up with the dew of heaven,
Then only Your presence can touch me.
Oh God, give to me faith that can fly.
I see storm and danger,
But my faith is an escalator of elevation
Loving on the only One who created creation.
Lord, give me You.

———◆———

THE JOURNEY

—◆—

Sometimes we spend our whole lives
Looking for truth on a highway of lies.
We spend hours striving for perfection
In the eyes of crooked hearts and the minds of those who feed on
refined imperfections.
Sometimes we find ourselves staring in the mirror,
Looking for a personal superhero
To end all that makes us feel inferior.
Sometimes we dream during nightmares and wake up in the losing
circle of someone else's reality.
Sometimes we await closure
That in one way or another encloses us in the past
And sometimes turns into some days
And some days turn into some years.
That we await an answer for this black hole of hopeless ambition,
But we are stuck looking for a restitution.
I found myself in a search for truth.
I found myself searching for life in dead situations.
I found myself suffocating on words with no substance,
And I found myself walking down a road afraid to turn back or push
forward,
Drained from the journey
And bruised from life's daily surgery.
I'm stranded in the middle of nowhere
With the keys still left and gears ready to be put in drive.
If I knew this would be a road of blind faith,
I would have worn a permanent blindfold.
But I'm starting to understand that's how my God-written story
unfolds.
I leave the key and pack up my bags.
I start down the road from the direction I believe I once came.
I lost people that I thought I'd never release.

I lost feeling in a place that I thought would never need filling.
I lost sight in the process of fighting my greatest enemy who belonged
to the inner me.
I lost the hope in the process of longing to be free,
And I lost the ability to see while staring at this man-made light.
Now one would think I'm incapacitated,
But I've acquired more illumination.
In these 21 years I've learned more in a day
Of this collegiate endeavor
Because I know there's truth in the phrase "pain doesn't last forever."
I packed up clothes that look like books,
Accumulated with dust and ripped pages,
To stand symbolic of the outdated memories
And growth stages that God wanted me to release.
I carry empty bottles or seemingly half filled,
Matching the level of achievements I've never fully eased.
I carry my written stories,
Not just in mind or heart—
They are etched across my exterior,
Reminding my body of its purpose to never go back to the start.
Where do I go with all these markings?
Where do I turn to?
Where isn't the question, rather, when?
With Whom?
And will I be ready once He says go?
I can only hope that the Painter of me
Is holding a beautiful masterpiece that goes beyond what life itself can
see.
I can only hope that what will be left behind
Will help others to live outside of the word
"Mine."
But I don't really know; I'm still on that journey,
Holding on to the words He breathed into me
And marching into a world that hasn't fully come to be.

BREAKING THE SILENCE

I felt it engulfed in my throat.
I felt it wrestle my tongue and strangle my vocal cords, like an
outgrown child's coat.
This was the day I realized
My words were powerless.
This was the day that words,
Once a solace place, died in an abyss of the unheard.
I remember trying to speak,
Every syntactic structure
Shattered like water against lava.
I was alone in the world,
And this killer of substance
Had jamboree into the power of my being.
Oh, how I dreaded the moments that await me.
Seconds became eyes of the never-ending sea,
Yet I decided to accept my stifle mutism.
As the hours of this suffocation
Tightened its grip,
I felt myself gasping for just a microsecond of breaths.
But whatever came in had already quickly left.
Now I am an aftermath
Of someone else's destruction.
If the same words I have now,
I'd had then, I would truly comprehend
What the birds grow instinctively to do:
Fly and soar.
With the grasp truly locking in,
I remember all the things I should have said.
I should have said "I love you" more.
"I'm proud of you."
"I appreciate all you've done."
But now those words are running against Usain Bolt,

And I believe the marathon of time has depleted all which matters
most.
Like a thief, the key to success lied on the taste buds of a strangled
muscle,
So I make my final vocal toast.
And through the clamped tension
I release forth an inner decision.
It rumbled in my belly as thunder does across the sky.
It shook my insides like a rhythmic earthquake.
I'm incapable of telling a lie,
But this feeling brought out a suppressed memory.
Seeing it flash across my eyes,
I felt tears of frustration,
Loneliness, and brokenness resurface.
Then all at once,
There I was again,
Laying in the captive dark room of my 10-year-old self.
I saw her sitting in the corner of the room,
Embracing the external scars
Which marked my parents' disappointment.
And on my tongue was the same suffocated ointment.
There on my body,
Etched on my skin, was moral disgust
And shame.
On my hands, hurt from this very being which carried my name,
I wanted to reach out and save me.
But I couldn't believe, with these new mature eyes,
I watched the 10-year-old me cry.
This cry first subtle,
Then determined and secure as a lion pronouncing its dominance.
As the cry was released,
I saw a mighty hand swoop down
And provide comfort.
I saw this being who possessed light
Beyond the charge of power distribution.
I wasn't too young to understand
That this form was no mere man.

But God, the One who created more than what we feel we control on
His land.
I watched as He unchained me from my personal bondage,
Then spoke these words:
"My daughter, I'm about to give you words
That have no bounds,
No faltered utterance,
But which possess substance beyond the rounds of humanity.
And with them I want you to understand that many will doubt the
meaning,
The very things you're feeling.
Know that in time these same words I've given
Will provide spiritual and physical healing.
Now get up."
Then He turned to me
And said, "You're free, I've given you the power.
Anything from Me is stronger than any fantasy or made-up belief."
Back to my reality,
I began to build up strength
Just to declare over myself:
No weapon formed against me shall prosper.
I am the salt of the earth.
If God is for me, then nothing shall stand against me.
As a leech loses its suction with salt,
Silence's grasp loosened like a victim freed of assault,
Now feeling my power regain.
Every unspoken word flowed like a stream with no end or beginning.
I spoke with only the intent of living.
I turned to face my oppressor.
Now face to face with her,
I could see the greatest opponent of mine
Shared my same mind.
Turning to confront this side with confidence,
My stance cracked the mirrored self-providence.
It was me.
I could see my eyes ached with pain
Which couldn't be measured through salinity of the ocean

Or the cure for heartbreak found in the bottom of self-made potions.
I saw on my body the lifeless words
That created its own melanin brand.
I saw the beauty of being broken,
But I couldn't become another lost soul or passed-around life token.
With the same words which choked me, I used them to redefine what
I see.
The mistake which weighed on you
Does not change what the Lord
Will or has done.
You will nearly lose your family,
Your hope, and your faith,
But for every anomaly
God will strengthen you to stand.
No matter what, this is a part of
His plan.
You will experience God's presence for yourself.
You will witness firsthand the power of His resurrection
As He revives the part of you which died.
You will reevaluate those who you feel are of importance.
You will lose the ones who said they'd never leave,
But in their absence, God
Will show you all you have to offer,
Giving you one chapter of many to come.
A graduate, top of your class,
Possessing the understanding on why
Time must always pass.
Closing that high school book,
God opened the door.
Now you're on a college campus
With favor and grace,
A new adventure afoot.
You will impact lives
In the same skin
You regretted that God never took.
They will look up to you
Because, through pain and struggle,

You've learned how to push past
And trust that God provides despite those who said you wouldn't last.
You'll have moments of disgust,
Moments of regret,
And moments of hurt.
Yet each will bring you closer,
Each will mature you.
You will be face to face
With your offender.
But you won't lose your place.
You'll swallow your rage
And continue to live out your reality days
Until you approach 21.
All the anger, hurt, and suppression
Resurfaces like a dormant volcano.
Now you make a lifetime confession.
"It wasn't my fault.
God, I don't want to carry this burden
Across my heart.
God, please forgive me.
If I could take it back,
I would.
If I could shout it across the rooftop,
I would.
God, I just want to be who You want me to be."
Each day onward, you start to love
On Victoria.

As I looked up,
The mirrored reflection
Looked different now.
She looked stronger,
Her bruises were gone,
Her demeanor was as radiant as the sun and her stance was of
someone
Born to run.
She smiled at me.
In her eyes I began to see
My past, present, and future.
I reached out to touch my mirrored self;
I was sucked into it.
Now standing on a stage
With many who shared this page,
Eyes glaring at this new form
I am created to be,
I spoke into the mic
And said, "Let God give to you a new day.
Break the silence of everything
And everyone that tried to change your outlook.
God is still in control.
I know because that's the story I just told."

———✦———

BATTLEFIELD

It's been said that all battles
Start in the facet of our minds
And grow to attack even the concept of time,
Then kills life as easy as fresh cattle.
But who would have known
That same battle of mind
Would place me on a land mine?
I was bounded by hands and feet;
I was surrounded by a type of light
Only understood at night,
And those around already
Had a death meet.
I have bruises that are now
Wounds etched on my heart
Or bleed on command.
I'm losing the strength to stand;
There are corpses everywhere.
No need to camouflage,
My battle has become my burial stage,
And the very air is intoxicating.
"Just give up, God doesn't care.
Just let go, come stand with me.
You'll never have any pain to bare.
I'll give you all your eyes desire,
But I need you whole, I need your mind,
Heart, and that soul."
He made it sound so sweet,
But I had a vow, I made at
My lowest, that I'd give my life
To the same Great One
Who saved mine.
So I dropped my head,

Not in defeat,
Rather, so he wouldn't see
My strength faltering.
As he tightened the chains,
I felt every bone
Crease in directions
Only plastic can truly own.
I started to cry,
But even my tears pierced
My skin.
I wanted to scream,
Yet there wasn't enough
Breaths circling inside
To revive this nightmare into a dream.
As my body slowly stopped,
I looked at the chains
Now crisscrossed over my arms,
Legs, and body.
Then with great pain,
I stared into the eyes
Of death, with just a whisper to say,
"May this same place be where my God's people never lie."
As my life started to dry,
I felt myself slowly die.
Just in a matter of seconds
He squeezed away my humanity.
"If I can't have you, then neither can He."

I felt it first as a fresh wind
Up the once aching crevice of what was me.
Then I felt a breath;
It had rejuvenated the cells that ceased.
I felt crushed bones
And organs reform.
I knew this could not be done
In life's surgery.
I wanted to look to see my doctor,

But the light He bore outshined
Every counted star in the sky,
And even if I wanted to touch Him,
My hands weren't strong enough to hold
This mighty blessed bold gift.
I wanted to hug Him,
But He radiated as far as the Pacific
To the Indian Ocean.
Such glory could be drowned in
If not fully realizing what is being shown.
I wanted to ask so many questions,
Yet during all my wants and thoughts,
He spoke:
"You must finish the work I have written.
I know what lies ahead are moments of defeat.
Remember Daniel was sentenced to be the lion's meat,
But I shut the mouths of the beasts and
Devoured the enemies who falsely
Accused him.
Remember that the glory you'll receive
Is always greater than the life you'll leave.
Remember that there's no fight
That My Light doesn't already outweigh in the gloom of night.
Get up, my daughter.
It's not over. Let's finish this."

Back in the position I started—
"If I can't have you, neither can He"—
I began to laugh.
"Don't be a fool.

You'll never earn the gift
That rightfully belongs to this Majestic King.
You will die in the same school
In which you trained your spirits.
These chains you've hung on me
Will be the same veins that suffocate all you thought you would be."

"It cannot be.
You should be dead,
Like all the others around you.
I shall have your corpse
As a trophy."
What you failed to realize is you don't have the last say,
And in my book
You never win;
You never stay.
Time and time again you lose instead,
So these chains can't contain me.
God said I'm free.
The chains broke down
And drooped like the scab of an old wound
With no purpose besides to let loose
The new skin that has taken form.
Every scar was gone,
And I felt my strength coming on.
"So, devil, tell me again how you lost the battle before,
Because I'm sorry to say this battle is still a victory of the Lord's."

———◈———

LOST IN TRANSLATION

My brother once said, "I'm lost and don't want to be found."
He is right
But then again wrong.
I see myself there,
However, finding my mind roaming.
With my soul in the air, waiting for
Justification for things unfair,
Revelations on every unclear affair,
Cancellation to all mental and physical scares.
Waiting for the world,
Waiting for humanity
To realize their master the Lord
And for their eyes to open to familiarity.
I'm so caught up with society,
And society is too busy detouring and blinding me,
Trying to make friends,
Then ending up breaking from the same word.
Letting the lyrical rhymes shake my mind, and trying to interrupt my
spiritual side,
Slurring the words "I love you"
As if the true meaning of love defines more than who.
Living to make it 'til tomorrow
But not knowing whether it will bring me sorrow.
Words speaking louder than actions,
Giving an unbalanced equation of infractions.
And who am I to talk
To see what others deny,
Then speak on it and still with no remorse walk?
I am more than a mediocre human
Who lies and deceives just to feel like part of a lucid band.
I speak past my time,
While people of my own are too bitter as lime.

And then I too am asked to become a speechless mime.
Living this life is quite revealing,
Yet too complex to easily prevail.
Daily one does the same thing,
And nightly the rhythmic consistency leaves an awful ring
Of what if, maybe, but never did.
Translate what,
When all is said and done,
Who will be left to transcribe
What was destroyed?
Translation,
Or a quick pick-up realization
That leaves one lost in glimmering isolation
And idiotic mesmerization.
Believing that the music I hear
Will help me relay my feelings near
And stop every heartache and tear.
Restlessly breathing in this process
When all things let go,
But I know I can somehow cross this.
This physical bridge between giving in
And staying strong,
Standing dead center as the bridge fights,
Disintegrating from left to right.
Where do I go when every possible direction is wrong?
How does one get up
When they have been down
And tossed around by stuff?
What is left when all is gone
And every path has been touched,
Yet never returned from?
Who remains when possessions are gone?
What is desire when nothing is gained?
Just perpetual fire.
Who flies solo when the wind has come to ease?
What is the aftermath?
Who will be solving it?

You live and learn.
You give and yearn
For things won and lost.
You and I hope for understanding,
Illumination,
On why things diverge,
Why our hearts can't merge.
What causes society to come at a standstill?
Where is everyone when you need to be healed?
Life leaves us with questions
That bring us to crossroads of what ifs and unwanted determination
To live to be the best
And to let our problems become tested then put to rest.
Life leads us down two paths
Between hope and faith,
Then the other for knowledge.
Faith that says through everything God is there;
That whatever may come I have no fear
Because I can bare.
And I know at the end
I have hope that there's more to me.

There's more God has for me to see.
Knowledge opens a world of desire,
Which leads to a life of unwanted trials
And no reason to believe in the impossible.
What is gained if you have all the knowledge in the world
But lose your soul, your sanity?
I lived this life caring
And breaking down, screaming
For you, society, friends, family
I have because I love.
Who? Everyone who has come into my life
And those who have stifled out.
I should just love Him,
God,
He who has transcribed all,
He who can stop time and I from falling,
He who builds up all that breaks,
Shakes, and shatters from mistakes.
He who knew me before I truly saw . . . Victoria.

THE ART OF LIVING

I ask myself, "What is life?"
Is it the ability to take a breath
Or have it exhaled by first inhale?
I ask myself if life
Is what makes humanity?
Then who determines vanity?
I ask myself if life is only bounded
By those who create their own crowns.
Why is it that rare jewels are found
Underneath the surface of death's tomb?
But they tell me to stop being negative
And to keep living outside my room.
What they don't know is I've lived longer,
In my mind,
Than those who write textbooks or memoirs.
Not saying I'm me reincarnated
But that God has shown
What He's always tried to illuminate.
Some just decided to see.
So I ask again, "What is life?"
And how can you tell me I'm not living?
We build up monuments to applaud those crushed in their crusades
of beliefs or endeavors,
Yet you will never see the appreciation for the only King.
You gave that to a man laying 6 feet under.
You tell me if I receive a degree
I'm guaranteed a position in my field
And a pay to match the academic struggle.
But you didn't tell me I'll fail or experience personal hell or reality will
thwart my dream.
All you said is to succeed,
You must have some type of degree.

But there has to be more to life
Than historical facts, mathematical equations,
Scientific theory, or grammatical errors.
Sounds like a world filled with social terror.
This world has shown me that love can be bought,
Not through jewelry but through young girls or boys.
Because the biggest crime is the mind's want.
The world has shown me its buried hurt
Which laid down many of my uncles and aunts.
Inside those graves lies bones that bare no pigmentation,
But now even in life or death the color of skin
Still seems to win.
What is life?
When living is comprised by escape rooms?
What is living?
When my brother doesn't speak?
Not because he's a mute
But because he recognizes the power of his words
Could not only free but restore.
Rather, save himself, he befriends his personal companion ole lonely.
What is life?
When those who believe are lost,
Not just in the world but in their hearts?
What is living?
When all around is on the verge of decay?
I believe life is art
Composed of different expressions,
And each figure playing their own part.
Only difference there exists only one Artist,
And as He etches the uniqueness (or "mistakes," as we may see),
Each angle eludes beauty no matter the form.
I've tried to put on glasses
To comprehend the beauty He sees
In this tragedy,
Yet no lens could fully focus
On the beautiful brokenness playing in humanity's parody.
Still, the Sculptor of man

Removed all my lenses
As He began to speak words as sweet as the angelic melodies:

"When I created man,
I gave to them the choice.
Even giving them the Garden of Eden,
Adam and Eve still desired more than what
They were seeing.
I, being the loving Father, let them decide which was greater to lose:
A taste of forbidden bliss
Or the ambience of my heavenly kiss.
They chose what was forbidden
When I already told them nothing is hidden,
Driving them from the first paradise built on Earth's land.
This is how the story of life and choice began.
Their disobedience and taste for more
Is the same reason today My people hide their shame as before.
I loved them despite their choice.
There are 66 books that express My accounts
But not just of Adam and Eve.
There are hundreds of stories to be found,
And to be precise, they're written from old to new.
But that wasn't enough.
I gave them My only Son,
Yet like a judge ruling the land,
They persecuted Him.
But My love resurrected Him as My Truth and Life
Just to show I'm the same no matter which way.
So, no, My daughter, I can't let you focus
On the brokenness of day,
Because even night has to go away.
I created man to worship Me,
Yet I find them knelt down counting bills,

Women and children scurrying across the floors,
And my people hiding in the hills.
I see beauty,
You see tragedy.
I see possibilities,
You see obscurities.
I see the heart of My people,
And you see color or face first.
I call for moments of rebirth;
Instead, you have picked up arms and ridicule the world I call Earth.
I see hope;
You see demise.
My people speak as if they have no vision.
They live as if I'm capable of sinning,
But by definition, I am Life.
Without Me, your breath can't be given.
So tell Me, do you know what it means to be living?
The birds don't sing
Unless I give them the voice.
The wind doesn't blow
Unless I release them to go.
There is no night and day
If I didn't open My mouth and say.
There is no you or universe
If I didn't appoint each alignment
And create the concept of birth.
You ask Me what is living?
Take My hand;
Let Me show you all I'm willing to give.
Your heart and thoughts are forgiven."

———◈———

GRACE CARD

The life I lived in a matter of years
Has unraveled through the heir of time,
For my name has become the foreground of my tears
And my physique, undoubtedly so permeated all
Which makes me unique.
I've become a victim to the standards of a world
I don't even belong.
I've become a shadow to my own shadow,
A stranger in the reflective sightings of myself.
In every mirror,
I've become enslaved to my own insecurities
Which uproot my moral compass and secure in me self-doubt.
Demoralized, criticized, lied to, and defiled,
Simply because who I am is composed into one
And doesn't dissolve into two:
One to your acclaimed standards,
The other to the One who classified me.
When the world said, "I deserve no distinctive class,"
God redefined me as one of His promised to last.
He held me when my backbone failed.
He guided me when my eyesight foresaw hell.
He loved me when I couldn't love me,
And despite the accusations, He took my sentence,
For He showed me grace.
I fell into a pit of self-pity.
I was submerged into a depressive city,
For I've seen my pains.
I've gone blind by the wounds I've gained,
But like the wind, God is constant.
Inside my self-pity, He gave me the Holy Ghost.
He rejuvenated my strength,
Made my pains reasons to rejoice for the rain,

And washed away the tear stains
To match my spiritual cleansing.
And just like that, He took me into His hands.

"For I am God.
I loved you before I created you.
I knew you before your name was chosen.
I wrote your story for My ultimate glory.
I've seen your struggles before they happened
To test your faith aptitude
And expand your reach, not only in longitude but latitude.
Not to break you down,
Not to see you consumed by even the faintest sound,
But yet another test of realization that I'm always around.
There's not a hair on your head that falls I didn't see.
There's not a headache that I didn't feel pulsing above your brow.
There's not a sleepless night when I didn't lie right next to you.
There's not a question too low that I didn't hear you murmur, 'How?'
For I've foreseen all before the day to come.
I felt the whips of My oppressors.
I carried the cross which bore the world's sin.
I kissed the pavement with blood and tears
Because the creations in which I love couldn't
Carry these scars.
Because no other could do what I've done:
Die for sins for which they didn't commit,
Be hated for truth underlining my blood.
So don't think I don't know your pain.
If it wasn't for My sacrifice,
This very world wouldn't exist.
No, there wouldn't be life.
I made it from night to day,
And you can't tell Me you've gone through enough.
You can't say you're free
Because you don't even recognize I've already freed Victoria.
I gave you victory as a birthright;
Life as a matter of free choice.

You feel your opposition is blocking My light.
Do you not remember My voice
Which spoke to you out of the silence?
Which called you daughter in the midst of the devil's
Evil malice?
Do you not remember I shaped you
From head to toe, specifically and uniquely?
Do you not remember I cradle you to slumber?
I made you a part of the number?
Do you not see me cleaning the mirrors?
I'm the one and only.
If there is no Me, there is no end
Or beginning.
Do you not remember there's nothing impossible for Me?
I made everything possible—look around, see.
I called you out of the world.
Don't you think I know they'll think your morals are absurd?
Just stay in My Word, and they won't stick around.
Stop playing the self-pity card.
Trusting in me isn't that hard.
I'm the giver of grace.
Many won't live to see 18 years
Or even live to see their fate.
Get up, My children, and walk in My great grace."

———✦———

WHAT IS FAITH?

Many people have their own definition,
But I'm going to give you a few perspectives,
And you can decide which fits the faith
Defense.
Faith is like pregnancy;
You don't push until you're ready
For deliverance or delivery.
It's like seeing a newborn baby open their eyes
For the first time.
To your surprise, they either smile or cry.
Reaction always tells if you're blind.
Faith is like growing a plant:
You position it for the perfect amount of light
And water daily, keeping it from harm
Or even from ants,
Not to consume it but so its beauty can consume you.
Faith is like dressing up for a party:
You sent out invitations,
But the only One who shows
Is an unknown "stranger" dressed head to toe
With an ambience that begs you to open up.
Faith is the sun rising and setting:
It starts the day with light
Then ends it with the same intensity.
It baffles me how we see God as a mystery.
Faith is not jumping just to fall;
Faith is taking that jump because you recognize where you are
Is too far from where God wants.
So you jump, knowing if you miss
He catches and protects you from every directed hit.
Faith is like a cloud
Filled with the power to restore or supply,

And sometimes it can overpower the reality of life in just one hour,
But it travels as far as you allow it.
Faith is like the birds and bees:
Even if there's a storm coming,
The instinct of fight or flight
Allows you to be prepared
Even if the odds aren't in your favor.
Faith is intoxication:
You can't just stop.
After the first hit,
Your body longs for an overdose
Of real love
To bring oxygen throughout.
Faith is a car ride:
It drives you to landmarks unseen
And connects the past with present
Just so you can arrive and descend as you please.
Faith is a bus stop:
No matter how many times you leave,
He shows back up to pick you up
Where you last walked off.
Faith is love:
It grows over time
And defines your character
To connect to others and God above.

Faith is the beating of a heart:
It is constant as long as you're consistent
In living with Him as your focus.
Faith is the cool breeze
On the hottest summer day,
Bringing a refresher when you've forgotten to breathe.
Faith is that light
Which shines throughout blackouts:
Yes, there are candles and flashlights.
This outweighs the wax
And outlast the batteries.
Faith is truth
Even when being dismissed, repressed, and deprived:
It breaks free despite all shackles,
Reminding you to always rise.
Faith is a defibrillator:
It revitalizes life that was pronounced dead,
Brings back beatings of a beaten soul
To return to a true Creator—not these fake imitators.
Faith is the key
To understanding journey and destination:
You can only fulfill one by complete separation.
Faith is what keeps me.

DEAR GOD

I possessed thoughts beyond my experience.
I felt feelings that matched not of me.
I was afraid to lie down and sleep,
For the unknown was uncomfortable,
And seeing the light amongst darkness
Was never truly inviting.
I spent hours fighting sleep
While thoughts of stretching beckoned me.
The doors of a foundation built on rock
Now unlocked its wall,
And like Noah leading the helm of the ark,
He flooded me.
Engulfed inside a storm of elegance,
Everything once relevant faded.
Inside a giant mammal of the sea
I can still see the soul of Jonah.
That prayer still echoed amongst
The bowel of its ringed intestinal tract.
Well, I don't know.
You told me the decision to follow You is simple
And I would become a disciple.
Then explain to me why I now have more loss
Than gain?
Explain to me why I'm enraged
By the very essence that makes me human.
Expect trials and tribulations,
But I'm tired of being tried and tested.
Let me test the test.
Let me switch position with my opposition
To redefine the juxtaposition.
Let me like the wind die suddenly
But rise like warm air does abundantly.

Speaking is like sandpaper
Cutting edges that wish not to be smooth.
And what am I supposed to do
When everything disintegrates like the morning dew?
Where is my peace
When I'm standing in a million pieces
Between a promise and comfortability?
Like a bridge connecting two pieces of land,
I'm torn between mandate and personal demands.
If I speak up, I'm tossed into a cell.
If I pray, I know my oppressors will feed me into their traps and
snares.
If I stand, I'm sure to be stabbed in the back.
But like the sun after day break, I rise.
Like the hanging leaf on a tree, I'll still break away and be free.
Like a predator waiting to feed upon its prey, it doesn't expect
Me to attack.
Yet its shock doesn't change instinct
To fight back.
Some days I feel like a routine puppet.
Some days I feel myself consumed
Inside the constipation of thoughts,
And like a snake slithering stealthily
Against the grains of the sand,
Our bond grows distant.
My heart still begging to ask,
Where has life inside me
Departed through the night?
Yet like an asthmatic patient,
I can't breathe without your permission
To inhale,
And I can't exhale without you
Giving me the pass to step out.
A past shell
Like a rose bud enclosed
Behind the potential to bloom,
Yet afraid of my time.

You said to me that I'm chosen.
You said to me that it wasn't I who chose you
But You who always chooses me.
God, why would You do all this
When my positional call
I still fall short of?
I have flaws which make
Me feel shorter than my actual being.
I have thoughts that linger
Longer than the stench
Bruised upon a heart or finger.
I have words that go without expression,
Lost in the conversation between
Suppression and confession.
Yet like a thief You've stolen
The sole jewel of my life:
Me.
You spoke into the thoughts
And transformed fantasy into
Actuality.
You gave purpose through the journey of broken reality.
There is gravity, but You gave me the sweetest love which bores into
my heart cavity.
You broke the laws of dynamics
And elevated my longevity
To outweigh the pressing of tragedy.
But Your heart is the reason my eyes
Will never understand beauty beyond the atmosphere.
Your vision sees past my present transgressions and gleams into me
Future pursuits and spiritual progression.
A dead girl I was knocking on death's door,
Hoping for him to be home.
I was ready to go,
And my tomb already made its bed
On the lifeless crevice of my room.
Yet like a mortician
You came to inspect what I had inside.

I was convinced I died,
But Your hand reached down
And placed in my very veins
Spiritual oxidation to understand
Life outside of my bodily cells.
I felt anew.
I felt I knew,
Yet just as I arise
I noticed flowers around my life wilted
And died.
That's the cycle we all must take before our fall.
It was then when it became like a sixth
Sense to me,
Seeing with my heart,
Young but not naïve.
A child turning from childish ways
To understand the path of life's day.
I noticed that these life lines are cordless,
And these frames of memory
Don't truly permeate what I see.
I noticed the grass
Through cemeteries' growth.
I noticed breathing is awakened
Through suffocation,
And yet You breathe life inside this mummified corpse standing
before You.
I see purity in brokenness
And beauty in hopelessness.
My heart breaks at those
Who lost the will to
Live.
Eyes once living now blinded by the
Orchestra of man,
Their mind lacks slumber
Like Florida showing any other emotion besides summer.
So I suppose heat will kill lust
Or regrow a new suckling virus.

God, those who died, are they free now?
Their souls confined between Earth
And senseless coffin worth?
God, when death hits close to my heart,
Is it purposeful?
God, I want to understand not the essence
Of life but why it's hard to stand when I feel like I'm always being
used.
God, I want You
Direly
Because I recognize only You can show me
What to do.

———✦———

MIRRORED TO SEE

Shadows exist in the day and night.
They outline and mirror
The shape of their leaders.
Whichever direction led,
The shadow follows.
Tell me, what do you see
When you look in the mirror?
Tell me if you can see what I do?
When you look in the mirror can you see the etched lines
The sculptor has shadowing you?
Do you see precision or indirect incisions?
Can you see it?
Can you see the beauty in the frame?
Can you see the purpose of your being,
Or in your name?
Can you see how Majestic God is to place thought into you,
Like a doctor studying the structure of DNA.
God saw fearlessness from the moment your cry broke out of the womb.
Purpose in the intertwining of Creator and creation,
I believe God intended it this way, but can you see it?
A painter holds the paint and brushes in their hand,
Yet the image across the canvas comes after a thoughtful stance.
God held you in His hand
And without hesitation
Envisioned you.
Like a victim suffocating from quicksand,
In just seconds, He formed past, future, and present you.
Yet the only drowning is in the ambience of God
Who ignites all things marvelous and speaks
Darkness into day.
Do you see it?

We hold our tongue from hurting the feelings of others,
But God spoke with such elegance and grace
That in all things living
He didn't withhold from any ounce of His glory,
Each being having its own origin
And story, but do you see it?
Well, what He's spoken about you:
You are flawed yet flawless.
You are clothed in everything He loves
Yet bathed in the skin of sin.
Destined for destruction,
But He gave restoration.
Your subtle drive for more
Is the reason why lust
Is a part of God's disgust,
And wearing a disguise
Is the reason He sees truth
In every lie, but do you see it?
False morales
Are the reason we have hundreds
Of all-you-can-eat specials
Promising a buffet of well-prepared meals,
Yet delivering half-satisfying food
And a higher pay than proper service.
But God picked through the order
And prepared for you
Something more than what can be bought with quarters.
Etched in the lines of your frame
Is submission to an immortal King
Which will fulfill the void of any unction

With a life of purpose and function.
Inside your veins flows
Blood,
Blood which oozed from the Promised Son
As He took a guilty sentence
When it was us who needed repentance.
This same blood was pierced from His side
And dripped from His hands and feet.
This same blood that
Spills across the operating rooms
Like the coronavirus
And pacifies the murderers in the broken kind of man.
This same blood that washes hands clean
Then connects child to mother to father
Or sister to brother.
But what about to the only King
Who reflects Himself in you
So when you stare into the mirror there's
No cracks?
There are reflective segments
Of beauty that need no cover
Girl.
And purpose in the edges of your frame,
God knew what He was doing
Because when God created the mirror,
It was the day
He started creating you.

———◈———

THE AWAKENING

It was during the late nights
When my thoughts played Pac-man with sleep.
It was in the early mornings
Where the moon drove my consciousness,
And it was in my eyes
I'd hold back tears of exhaustion.
You would think at my age
I would comprehend the importance of life having numerous pages,
But I'm still a child who loves to be held in the arms of her mother
And father.
I'm still a bud with a prospect of perspective
That isn't fully exposed.
I would like to think
The rays of sunshine
Are You reminding me to trust that Your plan will unveil,
And just as a smile forms,
The light is then consumed by clouds of gray.
This is how my days tend to stay.
Instead of letting the restlessness abuse me,
I use my few ounces of adrenaline
To focus on the few words found.
It's been said you can only know
Limits if you've reached heights.
You can only know depths
If you've lived amongst the floors.
You can only know success
If you've understood what it means to fail.
So here I am at the verge of ending a chapter.
I don't know what comes after,
But I do know that I'm afraid of disappointing You.
The ocean is vast in life,
Yet many have explored it and can't fully comprehend its bounds.

Lord, is that me,
A piece of Your plan slowly found?
I believe that in the mesmerized memorized magnetic motion of
silenced commotion
You've given me a piece of Your spiritual portion.
It took the Trinity to consume this mind, heart, and soul of mine.
I feel things I've never felt before
And see things that go beyond measures.
So I begin to value every second of Your presence.
I started to treasure Your voice in my ear.
Oh, loving God,
Elevators elate at elevations because they're fulfilling their existence,
But I enjoy Your elevation because, like an escalator, You move each
step in command
And await me to make each step in walking by Your side.
This feeling of constant motion
Gives me my daily dosage of devotion.
I'm compelled
To understand this beauty
Which radiates from Your Mighty Hand,
And I really haven't seen it all because it's created all of the land.
So I ask You, Mighty King,
What is Your plan for me?
I ask You, Mighty God,
To grant these eyes of mine to see
How my destiny goes beyond any limits
Society may place on the one named Faith.
God, I want more of Your glory.
I don't have to know, You're not finished writing my story
Because day by day I'm a living witness of Your glory.
I ask, Father,
Where would You desire me to go?
Not so I can say no, but so these feet of mine can prepare for rain,
hail, or snow.
I ask You, Father,
When do You want me to stay awake?
Not so I can make an alarm or time our experience, rather, so my eyes

can pull up the shades of exhaustion.
God, in those clouds of gray,
I still feel Your light breaking free,
Telling me You'll always stay.
God, in my sleepless endeavors,
Like a patient with a high fever,
My spirit is ignited by the words and visions
You've shown me.
Oh Lord, what a sweet delivery.
I feel peace in every situation of uncertainty,
For surely the Lord who makes no mistakes certainly has calmed the
raging sea with ease and perfection.
I could walk for days,
But knowing this mind,
It wouldn't stand still.
Knowing that You're driving these thoughts,
It would shift into third gear.
Lord, I feel even social distancing
Can't distance me from the social demands.
My ears demand of You,
My hands have felt heat
Which still lacked core resistance.
But with You, there's warmth in every instance
Of Your presence, no matter

Mountain or valley.
I can't tell if these words have driven
My consciousness
Or just the feeling of getting to know You.
God, if I fall asleep, will You be there?
If I stay awake, will You speak?
For there are days where the birds
Don't sing in the morning,
There are days where the world
Seems to be staring back at me
And moments where time itself mocks my eyesight.
Now I'm blinded by anything You want me to see,
And like the weight on an anchor
I feel sunken in the depths of my element.
I ask to understand these feelings,
But I've come to recognize that Your move is imminent.
God, if I close my eyes, will You show me?
If I hold my breath,
Will You awaken me?
Lord, wake this heart.
Where do we start?

———◆———

HEART CALL

There are days where I drive 26 miles
Just to sit in a parking garage
And think about the grades and experience
Accumulated on my files.
I stare out into the trees
And clouds.
I begin to envy these living sentiments,
Having so much content in fulfilling their purpose
Supplementing life
And storing or releasing water.
I'd give anything to feel such stride,
But here I am on a voyage that ends
With not an alarm
Or speedometer
But with the everlasting beat of this heart of mine.
I suppose you can say I should be dead
In this world of the alleged living,
When we suppress thoughts of thanksgiving.
With paychecks of endless labor
And stepped-upon greed on fervent dreamers.
You ask me what's my purpose,
And I'll tell you my worth could range from a gold mine
To the taxable fee of pennies.
You can ask me what makes me unique,
And I could tell you I'm like the highway:
Connected but not truly intertwined
To one exact precise destination.
You can ask me how I feel,
And I'd tell you,
How does the sun feel on a summer day
When it's devoured even the clouds,
Then bites upon the few fresh breeze as it may?

You can ask me as much as you'd want,
Yet that wouldn't change these devilish taunts.
I could ask you why, if the sun and moon
Are partners,
The sun leaves before the moon comes,
And the moon can't stand to see the sun
Be the day starter?
Why is it that death and life
Runs in pairs, but joy dies
When tragedy joins the meet?
Why is there never enough purity
In one drop of rain,
Or truth built inside the facade of man?
Why is there a circumference
Of circumstance
But never a circumcision of cultivated cult culture?
Why would a good God
Go beyond the facets of this mind
To embrace the mechanical infractions
Under His creation's heart hood?
Why would a good God allow pain
When all we want is to remain sane?
Why would a good God
Meticulously plant seeds upon the earth
Just to see them wither away in the dust?
Why would a good God
Create such beauty during devastation?
Why would a good God?
Why would a good God?
Because He's a Good God.
A Good God who sees past my mileage
And sees me with a key
That grants me with a degree.
A Good God that instills purpose despite the world's effort to mask
my steps as worthless.
A Good God who, through love,
Allows us to see whatever may come.

There's still good which exists amongst the few some
Who, through the deaths
And slander,
Still yearn for that same breath
Breathed into Adam then Eve.
I'm telling you, He remembers you and especially me.
This same Good God
Who knocks on the heart of what He already knows,
Waiting for the day for us to open our eyes
To see who our true Lord is.
He who summons the stars in alignment
And orchestrates the waves by unique salinity refinement.
This same God
Who waits like a fisherman
For His souls.
No, He's no death or grim reaper.
This is the one who is my Soul Keeper.
I ask you this: if you knew
There was someone who had everything
In the palm of His hand
Which would transform you, who sees
Into parts of you you'd never know,
Would you follow Him?
If I told you there was someone
Who only has the best for you,
Would you settle for someone who doesn't match His intensity of great
Just because the others charge a lesser rate?
If I told you that this same someone
Who saw you at your worst
And waited for you to see the prize
Is better with Him running the course?
If I told you He desires
Your return more than humanity
Desires oxygen,
Would you believe me because of all I said
Or because you heard Him call?

THE POSITION

I watch the sun rise and set.
The moon shines then rests,
Day after day,
Week after week,
Month after month.
God, I'm not questioning You.
God, I'm not doubting Your move.
God, I just don't know what to do.
I've played tic tac toe with the very backs of those who vowed never
to turn.
I've played messenger to the walls
Of empty hallways
And on the crevice of fresh wind.
You've brought heat that exceeds the longevity of my skin
Now torn between stagnation and elevation.
I listen to the screams of silence
And hope that You can speak to me.
As a bird left to take flight,
I reach out to You during this spiritual and physical plight.
Conversations have muted on my end.
Those whom I've grown fond of
I find myself running away from,
And even strangers seem to mock my presence.
I wonder if this is what Moses felt
When he returned with the 10 Commandments,
Just to see the people turn their face from You.
I wonder if those stones that pierced Stephen
Were the same ones I walked on.
I wonder if the tomb that tried to suffocate Lazarus
Is the same reason why cemeteries have more attendees than rallies for
Jesus.
But God, I'm still waiting on You

Through sweltering heat.
I wait for You through the random rain bands,
Not to just feel Your Loving Hand in mine,
But I want my story I tell to
Reflect this faith stand.
Pressed against the asphalt
I'll blame myself,
Not the faults of the earth.
God, remember when I was a little girl
I used to dream about being a chef,
A fire fighter, a doctor?
And eventually the dreams stopped;
The thoughts ceased.
Eventually I searched for a reality in Your heavenly essence.
I found heart in the words spoken to the prophets.
I felt love in the tear stains of my words,
Yet You visited me often.
You laid next to me in hours of mourning
Where I felt alone and left unheard.
You showed me my past reality
Reflects my present parody,
Even in my short-lived journey.
You stayed and said, "Let me hold thee."
You held with a grasp
That would crush the Earth.
Instead of destroying, it mended the halves
Of my heart,
And in a matter of seconds, I understood
What it meant when You said everything has its timing.
I felt strength that energized every cell in my body.
I felt a breath more satisfying than oxygen.
Ooo, but God, Your love became my drug.
I was hooked and addicted.
This addiction brought about physical evictions, spiritual
commitment, and mental sedation.
Torn between this intoxicating fantasy
And a lifetime of tragic reality,

I fell hopelessly in love with the very thought of You.
You are divinity.
Each second of life feels infinite,
But knowing tomorrow could be the day
I stand before Your throne to spend eternity,
I'll avoid sleep just to hear Your final say.
God, the solemn silence of mourning
Is the reason why night
Falls and I can't tell.
The silence of You
Is the reason my shadow shadows
And the reason why the beating of my heart
Has no start or restart.
The silence of You
Is the reason why these eyes
Have lowercased the noun of I.
The silence of You
Is why the clouds of day
Drive my mind Your way.
The silence led me to a searching soul.
There, she was on the brink
Of eternity and the exit of society.
Engulfed in frustration
And fear,
She wanted death to be her
Only friend.
I saw her breaking as day does from night,
Yet this breaking was shattering,
And she would scream
If pain hadn't stolen her freedom of speech.
Clinging onto the edge,
Tears cut the frame of her face
As she prayed this decision be what
Brings her internal peace.
She lifted her body onto the ledge,
And like a defendant of America's
Allegiance,

She stood to face her accuser.
I wanted so badly to switch positions with her,
But as I pressed closer,
My steps caused her to tremble.
I stretched to touch her,
And I felt hurt engrossed in years
And years enveloped in a disease
Of unforgiveness.
She turned to face me.
Then I could see it clearly:
Across her face were those who
I bypassed and had yet to reach.
As the faces flashed by,
I stood heartbroken
At the lives wanting
To hear what God has spoken.
I knew the decision they wanted to do,
But I refused to let them die.
God, save them.
God, create in me a vessel.
A vessel that speaks as You orchestrate.
A vessel that leads by a set-apart example.
A vessel that loves without boundaries.
A vessel of the Lord.
In opening my eyes, she's gone.
Now I'm on the ledge.
Then He said, "Take your position.
I've brought you too far to watch you fall.
Shift into position.
The world is accusing you,
But in My eyes, you are excused.
Walk into your destiny.
All that awaits is Me."

———◈———

CAGED BIRD

I hold onto small ounces of light,
Hoping that, in the midst of this,
It would fight the thoughts and feelings
I've become accustomed to wearing.
You wouldn't notice because it's become a part of me,
And even if I showed you,
You still couldn't see
All that I fight against belonged to my genetic make up.
I'm estranged to the reflection in the mirror—
A fool to those who see me as a hero.
Don't ask me what I feel
Because fillings are for those who have cavities,
And these voids can't be filled.
They're unrepairable holes.
I am a bird trapped in this cage.
There's no reason to lock me down,
I've already chained down my own pain to my living stage.
You don't know my pain.
You hear about it across the fragments of my temple
But know not the frame outline which detours my existence to be
anything but simple.
You admire my beauty and intellect,
But can't you see the beast of my emotions on the surface
Or the thoughts of freedom running through my mind like a rogue
renegade for allegiance?
I would ask you to free me,
Yet these locks are constricted by the lifeline blocks of me.
I'm not asking you to see,
I'm telling you I need to be free.
I never understood how animals in captivity could readjust their
minds to defer from freedom,
Each day restricted to certain steps, meals, and the occasional visitations.

As I look at myself, I now see
It isn't hard to reinvent life outside of a cage,
Especially when you're the one with the ball and chain.
These bars refraining my growth,
I see as sections of my life I wish to not touch—
Not because I don't understand,
The past prepares the present to create a future—
Rather, some things just have a stronger pull on my worth.
I know I'm not alone,
But why does it feel as if I'm the only one searching
For answers in a desert of my situations' clone?

It doesn't get cooler through the day.
This desert heat scorches, with each turn I sway.
I can't tell you if I can hold on.
The fight leaves me in each wave,
And I'm tired of hoping that anyone will be brave to save me.
In the non-consistency of life, I've become a constant resistance
Through the few seconds of happiness held in an instance.
I don't expect you to understand.
I don't find it surprising if this plea gets the demand of not one single
woman or man.
So just leave me where I am.
I still have the strength and ability to stand.
Like the poachers of ivory, watch my strength get sliced from outside,
Then inside.
But this won't break me.
I'll still stand.
I am a stranger to you,
But a friend, Father, and future for others.

"I am yet a stranger to you,
But you are not a stranger to Me.
I've sat in your prison cell,
Morning to night—
Or should I say night to noon—
And I've watched tears only apparent to the moon

Flood the screws of your cage
And heard you replay freedom melodies
Through the frontal cortex of your brain.
No, you haven't gone insane.
For every situation without limits,
It's in Me that even in darkness light still emits.
I could break these chains;
I can free you.
But as I've said, you don't really know Me.
So daily I wait for the key,
Not to your cage but that heart which beats beneath the ribcage of
your existence,
Just to exercise My heavenly love
On your dire emergency.
But like many of My creations,
You haven't seen what I have in store.
And like an author of a soliloquy,
I know what you don't.
I take away what you won't.
I hold what can't be touched.
I place more than what feeds the greed of many at lunch.
I free what others can't dare to dream.
I am the living God, although many say I'm a fantasy.
So no, I'm not asking you to give up.
I'm telling you that even a full cup
Knows when it had enough.
There's still work ahead.
Take My hand; let Me free you from this emotional affair.
Let Me give to you freedom
That frees the very substance you call air.
Let Me answer your injustice
With the solution that gives to you resolution and new substance.
Nothing I create remains in chains.
Let Me create the very means for your change
Because little, little bird, all from you is already heard.
Walk with Me from your cage."

SILENT PRAYER TURNED VICTORY DECREE

———◆———

God, I,
God, I,
God, I,
Just forget it.
But God,
I told myself I wasn't going to do this.
I told myself that this too shall pass.
I told myself that this is all a part of Your plan.
I told myself that each test and trial,
You were the only reason I stand.
And in each moment of defeat,
It was by Your grace I could still get
Up from these great feats.
And with You, I only follow Your feet.
So I didn't say it.
I didn't say how I wanted to run away.
I wanted to close my eyes,
And like Humpty Dumpty, have a great
Final fall
Because, God, every time I reach for Your hand,
The very school curriculum suffocates our
Matrimony band,
And when I open my mouth to speak,
Words once loud, vibrantly clear,
Beckon inaudible and meek,
So God, I started to silently pray,
I hid my tears in the dark
And my exhaustion in my heart.
I couldn't understand,
And eventually pursuing this collegiate

Purpose wasn't of high demand,
It left me feeling worthless.
I looked up to heaven, hoping to see
Beauty during the storm,
Yet You sent me more heat,
Then eventually rain.
What more am I to do
When all the grace and favor You've shown
Has become nothing but an empty form?
God, I go to class daily,
And what is learned I vaguely remember.
I'm just waiting for the month of December.
I want to be an example,
But it seems as if the more I say it,
The devil makes me one of his destroy samples.
I silenced this prayer of help for so long.
I assumed I was doing something.
God, when I put on this ring,
It's symbolic to ten years of unconditional love,
And I know this is all conditional
And testifying about You,
And I know it isn't good enough.
So God, I need Your love and presence from above
Because the rings around my eyes
Are retelling the tiredness I disguise.
That same pain is starting to show,
For I know Your answer is, "Hold on,
I'll show."
But God, all around me is silent,
Which has destroyed the seldom solace soaring and scaring my secret
attack to my spirit and soul.
God, awaken me from my sinking opposition,
Or am I living in my final prayer petition?

While taking my defeat,
You made Your presence known,
And said, "Let me speak."

"My daughter,
My daughter,
Do you know Me?
Have I not given to you eyes?
So, through Me, I'll show you
What the devil doesn't want you to see.
You see only your struggle
And what's in front of you.
I see the before, in-between, plus after scenes.
I see your opposition,
And it's not your final position.
For every new position
I've foreseen and created so I can get the
Glory not once, or twice, but
Throughout your entire life.
Each trial you experience
I already know the outcome,
I just need you to hear My voice
And come.
I have the keys to your success,
So let Me give them to you.
I want every quiz, test, and class
That the devil placed in your mind
That you won't pass.
I want every fear of self-doubt
To be sent back out your mouth.
Open your prayer up and out
Because amid it there's a shout.
My daughter, there is nothing on this earth
That is silent, for I hear all, even when you don't speak.
Haven't I, in twenty years, shown you blessings
In disguise and raining from the sky?
Haven't I told you I got you?

I hold you so close to My heart.
You don't even see My hand
Reaching for you from the start.
Yes, I know you want to achieve,
You want to succeed
And show the world what they thought
They conquered.
But, My daughter, your only job is to trust
And believe in Me.
Look around,
Look at the campus,
Look at the students,
Look at the course curriculum,
And most importantly, look at you.
You let your surroundings try to redefine
What I already declared
As victory.
I already have every result.
Some may say that's luck,
But they don't know my favor
Isn't categorized in secular superstitious stuff.
They don't know that I'm the only One
Who can flip a losing streak
Into a mechanical mistake.
So your only job, My dear,
Is to keep your eyes on Me.
Let your faith see
There's not a promise I don't keep.
Just go
So all can know
You have the victory."

———◆———

IN THE MIDST OF QUARANTINE

I look outside the barred window
And see silent streets,
No kids playing,
No birds singing,
Just a few cars placing their feet down.
But there's never much sound
Anymore.
I know there's still life,
But can I really say that when
It feels as if the world has hidden itself?
Has lost answers in their pursuit to be found?
The very fabric of humanity
On the verge of insanity
Because of greed and vanity.
I am not a prisoner to your fear.
These window panes
Will not withhold what I'm created to expel.
These walls of security are only restrictions,
If I had a specific category.
Why did God call me out for His glory
If I was meant to be contained?
Why do these same boundaries and chains
Fail to change me?
If I'm something the world tends to save,
Explain to me why outside of these four walls
I'm slaughtered at the door,
And every failed attempt is plastered on billboards and ridiculed in
the mention of every call?
If you knew what you tried to contain,
Would you make me into a lab rat

Or try to comprehend my existence going beyond the Census mat?
But of course, you can't bring quality into an environment that only
looks at quantity.
So here I am in quarantine.
I have a list of assignments
With deadlines that never end.
But none of these efforts of a degree
Bring reassurance or refinement.
I miss the wind kissing the leaves free.
I miss laughing with friends.
I miss the bipolar weather of sunshine,
Rain, and a few days of a cool breeze.
I miss driving the great interstate,
Not to just interchange speeds,
Rather, to feel my car fulfill her fate,
Racing the margins as if our destination is her only date.
I miss spending hours on a campus.
The level of stress and anxiety made all feel as if we were a family.
It wasn't just about you or me
But us.
I can't tell you if fear or the virus
Is the real killer.
All I know is time will reveal
We never know how long we have
Or when the world will officially heal.
So with the mindset of an engineer
And a spoken word believer,
I see to it that I live my life
With a heart knowing that God
Always hears.
God, will You save this world?
God, will You cradle those who
Suffer by this virus at hand?
Let us know to continue to stand.
The greatest gift we all are given
Isn't found out of our homes
But is built inside us from the moment

Our bodies took their form—
And that's the ability to love.
Let not this tragedy switch your focus
From what God intended life for you
Or even for I.
This is part of God's plan.
Dear people, don't let this quarantine
Subdue you like quicksand.
Take God's hand.
Let Him heal this land.

———✦———

A TRUE FATHER

It all started before the words I've written
In a land once belonging to just a King.
He crafted the heavens
Then called forth the Earth.
With the calling came the land,
Night and day,
And with just utterance separation of the vast ocean
From the sky.
This King saw beauty in His design
But still had more purpose to bestow.
He envisioned life of plants, animals, and humanity.
It's safe to say, this King
Lacked thoughts of vanity.
The life He formed in His vision
Would worship the very voice of Him
In spirit and truth.
Yet like a true ruler,
He gave His subjects a choice
Of their life to live:
Whether a servant to His freedom
With provision, hope, favor, and grace,
Reigning without cease,
Or a life dressed for the taking
But bathed in oppression, greed, and malice,
Just wanting only what appeased the eyes.
This King watched what was created
Try to overthrow Him as the creator.
Like a father releasing his rebellious child,
How can you embrace what doesn't want
Your love?
But the King released
His creation, His love, His child.

It broke His heart to watch their defeat.
He could have easily summoned them again.
All it would take is one knock,
One small or large loss.
An infinite cycle of uncertainty,
But He didn't intend on luring them in through deaths.
He wanted their submission to come with ease,
Not just because He begged for them to see.
This King and now Father
Waited for His children to come back.
There are 66 books He had written,
And to this day it is disputed on whether
They are fables or truths.
But if the world would take off their blinders,
It can be seen that those books
Tell of the beginning of how this amazing King
Created you, you, you, and me.
Despite His plan for man,
There was Adam,
But Adam couldn't take charge
And blamed Eve,
Depriving us of a garden
Where the King abides.
Humanity's choice was still to leave.
Abraham is the father of many nations,
But even through his obedience
The deeds of his seeds still turned from God.
Yes, they outnumbered the stars in the sky.
Now I see why

Each is farther from the Son.
Jacob worked years for a love that couldn't be found,
Stealing the right of firstborn.
His first choice for love was a trick
Turned maiden.
Saul the first proclaimed king
Let the people's thoughts
Drive him from sane to insanity.
There are so many more accounts,
But in the end
It took the manifestation of Himself in human form
To show how great love can go.
How He was willing to win over what was loss
By giving up Himself—
An innocent man with the world's sentence.
He gave His spirit,
Yet no one came to visit.
He brought grace,
Yet they slapped Him in the face.
He called forth revision
In His own image,
Yet many weren't willing.
A King and Father
Died alleged "sinner"
So our lives can go back to the One
Who said, "It is finished."

———◈———

MOUNT SINAI

Sleepless nights
But sleepy mornings.
Sleepless nights
But sleepy mornings.
Am I imagining this cycle,
Or has this cycle recycled me to
Believe day is night
And night has its own say?
I'd sing a song if the words did come,
But whatever is there has become an uttered hum.
I'd write as most good poets do,
But I don't feel like storytelling.
I find solace in the space of You.
And in
Minutes turns to hours
I feel elevation
That allows the thoughts of a caged bird
To soar even without flapping.
I come to know much,
Yet I don't know enough.
I learned purpose, stride, and vision
Through the brokenness of love and pain,
From friends turned enemies.
But most importantly I learned
Truth, love, and faith
Through the One who
said I am that I am.
In a matter of months
I lived more than 23 years.
I watched the change in degrees
Turn minds into triggers
And tongues into bullets.

I watched alleged soldiers
Show true skin of camouflaged affiliation.
I heard words of deceit
Falter under the light of day,
But they told me I'm too young to understand,
And I don't have much in-depth experience
To decipher black, white, or even gray.
Then explain to me why
It's easy to see truth bounded
Through restless nights
Rather than with the eyes of the weak.
I want to believe that what I'm feeling
Goes beyond the air blowing from
My ceiling,
But there's a breeze sweeping
The very bones of me.
There's a level of breaths that can't capture
The life inside this new formed heart.
I feel valves breaking.
Is this my Joshua chapter?
I've wrapped myself in this love known as Alabaster,
Yet I'm untamed to the thoughts of renegade.
Do I jump when the ledge is right there,
Or do I lay down still as night?
Unsure what to do, I just stay
Inside this man-made cave,
Sheltered and confined,
Comfortable behind the scenes of me.
For each day the battle rages.
It is not I who fails but them
Who fail to trump my victory.
It's hard to see growth when you're stunted.
So, on my knees I pray for direction.
In this pray-fed confession
I hear the wind beat itself against
My prayer closest,
Yet I know my God's movement.

I felt the ground beneath my sleepless quarters
Stomach rumble,
But no shaking could move me.
I hear fire screeching from heaven to Earth.
This fire is not my ignitor; it is a physical temptation on testing what
He can do.
But I've seen and know what this marvelous Being
Can create.
Hunched over, eyes peeled open,
My ears yearning for His voice
To pierce through the breaking of cycles
I know I have to be free
To lead others out of their Exodus.
But even Moses let what he'd seen
Destroy the handwritten commands.
I pressed my ear onto the floor,
Not to be rumbled by the people's lead,
I want to hear the King when He enters.
In the midst of pressing,
A still, soft voice
Echoed through the cave.
Its power brought me upright,
And just as Lazarus was awaken from
Death's tomb,
He broke through.
My hands followed the hips of the cave.
My feet in-tuned with musical steps
Raced on this straightened ground.
Reaching the opening,
There awaits a light.
This light carried such conviction.
My very being dropped its usual subscription,
And what was once weight
Fell from my shoulders.
The restraints of control

I wanted so badly to fly away with Him,
For my strength has gone with the years
And my stance flooded in tears.
But just as the light brings joy,
He reminded me of what's to come:
The endless cycle of trials and tribulation
Which will destroy many and some.
He reminded me of His presence
That woke me from an abyss of hurt.
In Him no weapon shall ever work.
He reminded me of His love
Which bathed my heart whole.
Oh God,
He reminded me of His grace.
Days where this face
Forgot the truth I didn't deserve to taste,
He reminded me of this blood
Which flows once dripped on the floor.
Innocent yet cleaned, mankind's guilty core.
He reminded me of this mountain,
The place which brings glory
Like an everlasting fountain
To restore those who ask for help.
He reminded me of His plan,
Not of my ambitions or wants
But filled with victory through even my history.
And in moments I couldn't stand,
He reminded me of the place
Where I first decided to receive Him.
It was in my heart.
Now come and let me fix all the other parts.

DIVINE LOVE

I remember when I first felt Your eyes on me,
It made me smile.
Who would have known that You
Could see
Beauty
On this imperfect page of work?
I remember when You first touched my hand.
It was something that chemical bonds
Couldn't equally balance or understand
Because You fit perfectly in the voids
I didn't want to fill.
You took the holes and healed my soul.
I remember the nights
You crept into my room
Like a silent shadow.
You made it clear that You were staying
And opened my heart's window
As you placed Your presence
Where I was laying.
It was in Your arms
I felt love that I never wanted to omit.
I felt a haven
That those who never felt You
Truly don't understand: what it means to be worth saving.
I remember our early morning talks.
You spoke with such life,
Love, and passion for this heart of mine
That I would lose track of time,
Captivated in the gentleness and uniqueness You possessed on things
That cut through me like a knife.
But every day I fell in love with You,
Not because You forced Your love on me;

Rather, it was Your love for me that allowed
The perspective in my eyes to see
Genuine love in this amazing phenomenal You.
And as You pursued after me,
There were days where I was breaking,
Feeling the weight of our love getting taken.
So I hid; I avoided Your calls and texts,
As if Your voice and presence could be translated through these
relative objects that seize time.
Yet You showed up to say no, matter where I go,
"You'll be mine."
Speechless as a lover who
Only knows how to mime my reactions,
I decided to truly give into my heart's satisfaction.
I gave You my mind
So You could see the thoughts of memory
That don't comfort me.
I trust that in Your hands You'll show me joy despite this visual pain.
I gave You my sight
Because I've looked for miles for answers
On this set of footprints which always walks alongside me, morning,
noon, and night.
Now I can see it's always You.
I gave You my hearing.
These ears have heard stories that even the dead haven't told,
Yet You took what I've heard and said, "Sometimes you have to walk
into what's already foretold."
I gave You my heart,
Despite the factors and elements
Which try to annihilate each beat.
Your heart has built spiritual vents
That suck in the hurt and send it back
To the One who felt.
You and I would fall apart.
I gave You my soul
Because in a matter of seconds, minutes, hours, days, weeks, months,
and years,

You are the only Divine Love
I've known as my Lord.
There's no other who could do and say
All I've already shown.

———◇———